Wolves

Story by Mike Graf

Illustrations by Julian Bruère

Rigby PM Plus Chapter Books
part of the Rigby PM Program
Ruby Level

U.S. edition © 2003 Rigby Education
A division of Reed Elsevier Inc.
1000 Hart Road
Barrington, IL 60010 - 2627
www.rigby.com

Text © 2003 Thomson Learning Australia
Illustrations © 2003 Thomson Learning Australia
Originally published in Australia by Thomson Learning Australia

10 9 8 7 6 5 4 3 2 1
07 06 05 04 03

Wolves
    ISBN 0 75786 892 4

Printed in China by Midas Printing (Asia) Ltd

Contents

CHAPTER I

Howls in the Night

Ah ooooo ... Ah ooooo ...

Kaitlyn sprang up in her sleeping bag.

Ah ooooo ... oooo ...

She sat and listened to the eerie howls outside her tent.

Ah ooooo ... There it was again. "Dad?" Kaitlyn whispered, her heart starting to pound.

Ah ooooo ... oooo ...

"Dad?" Kaitlyn whispered again. She turned toward her father. But all she heard was a little snore.

Slowly, Kaitlyn slipped back down into her sleeping bag. She pulled the covers up to her chin and listened to the howling.

Ah ooooo ... ooo ... Ah ooooo ... ooo ...

Kaitlyn shut her eyes, then opened them. Her heart was beating wildly. She shut her eyes again.

Her father moved.

Kaitlyn opened her eyes and whispered, "Dad?" But he didn't answer. Kaitlyn shut her eyes again. Her breathing slowed down.

Ah ooooo ... oooo ... oooo ...

She listened and listened and ...

CHAPTER 2

Heaven's Peak

The warm sun shone through the tent. Kaitlyn turned over and opened her eyes. Dad was gone. She quickly sat up, got dressed, and scrambled outside.

Dad was flipping pancakes on a small gas stove. "Good morning, Sunshine," he said.

"Hi, Dad," Kaitlyn replied. "How'd you sleep?"

"Great! I didn't wake up all night. Are you hungry?"

Kaitlyn sat on a large rock next to Dad. He handed her some pancakes and a bottle of maple syrup. She soaked her pancakes in the syrup, and ate them hungrily.

Dad yawned and stretched. "Ah! There's nothing like the great outdoors. It sure gives me an appetite!"

"You always say that," laughed Kaitlyn.

"Because it's true," Dad answered. "Hey, are you up for a nice long hike today?"

"Is that the mountain you want to climb?" Kaitlyn asked, looking up at the jagged peak towering above their campsite.

"That's the one," Dad answered. "Heaven's Peak. I haven't climbed it since I was a ranger here in college. So – are you up for it?"

"Sure, Dad. I can't wait to see the view. I've heard so much about it!"

CHAPTER 3

"See You at the Top!"

"I'll see you at the top!" Kaitlyn called down to Dad. She scrambled up the last few feet of the rocky slope.

When she reached the summit, Kaitlyn looked around. Surrounding the mountain were deep green forests. Small lakes were scattered about in the wilderness far below. Distant mountains were speckled with snowfields and tiny glaciers. There were no signs of people anywhere. Now she knew why her father had talked about this place all these years. It was incredible!

Kaitlyn pulled her camera out of her pack and snapped several photos of the view – and of her father trudging up the last few feet of the trail. "Now everyone will know who got here first!" she laughed, as she took another picture.

Dad finally huffed his way to the top, and wiped the sweat from his brow. "Phew! I'm not as fit as I used to be."

"Yeah, Dad!" Kaitlyn joked. "You're not getting any younger, you know." She looked at his stomach. "You'd better start watching what you eat!"

"I watch every bite!" Dad patted his belly. He set down his pack and took out a granola bar. "Do you want one?"

"No, thanks," Kaitlyn replied.

Dad circled the summit and gazed out over the mountains and forests of the park. "Glacier National Park," he sighed. "It's still as beautiful as it was twenty years ago."

"What did you do when you were a park ranger here?" Kaitlyn asked.

"I studied the large animals of the park, like bears, moose, elk, mountain lions, and deer," Dad explained. "I hiked all over these mountains, observing wildlife."

"It would be so cool to work here!" said Kaitlyn.

CHAPTER 4

No More Wolves

The wind whistled over the summit of Heaven's Peak. Dad and Kaitlyn stood together, looking out at the distant mountains. Far below, the sun glistened on Two Medicine Lake.

Dad broke the silence. "I could stay up here all day."

"How about a photo, Dad?" Kaitlyn asked. "Stand right there. No, move a little to the left," she added, while peering through the lens. "There. That's perfect."

Kaitlyn snapped the picture, then let the camera dangle from her neck. She wrinkled her nose. *"Eee-ewe."* She waved her hand in front of her face.

"What?" Dad asked. "What is it?"

"Just don't step to your left," Kaitlyn answered.

Dad looked down. "Oh!" he exclaimed. A few inches from his foot was a large pile of animal droppings. "Hey, that looks fresh." He bent down to get a closer look. "That's interesting. It has fur and bones in it."

Dad stood up. "I wonder ..." He glanced back down. "No – it can't be."

"Can't be what?" Kaitlyn asked.

"At first I thought this might be from a wolf. But wolves don't live in this park any more. They were hunted to extinction in this area over 80 years ago. So that must be from a coyote." He headed toward the trail.

"Coyote?" Kaitlyn repeated, following Dad. "I guess that's what I heard last night."

"Last night?" Dad spun around.

"I can't believe the howling didn't wake you up!" Kaitlyn exclaimed.

"Howling?"

"Well, that's what it sounded like."

"Are you sure it didn't sound more like yipping?" Dad asked. "Like this: *Yip! Yip!*"

"No, I would say it was more like this: *Ah ooooooo ...*" Kaitlyn howled.

"Hmm," said Dad. He started walking again. Then he stopped and cupped his hands around his mouth. "Wolves?" he yelled. "Are you out there? Hey, *wolves!*"

"Wolves ... wolves ... wolves ..." echoed back from the mountains.

"*Wolves!*" Kaitlyn shouted.

"Wolves ... wolves ..." the mountains replied.

"Oh well." Dad shrugged. "Let's head back to camp. I'm getting hungry, and I feel like snacking on something."

"Already?" Kaitlyn laughed.

CHAPTER 5
Paw Prints

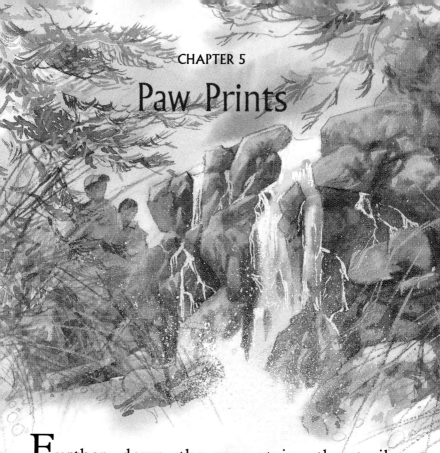

Further down the mountain, the trail entered the forest. Thick trees blocked out most of the sun and sky. Kaitlyn led the way as she and Dad hiked along in the early evening shadows. Tall grasses surrounded each side of the trail underneath the trees. A small stream cascaded across the trail, then tumbled down some rocks on its way to a lake below.

"Hold on a second, Kaitlyn," Dad called out, pulling off his pack. He took his cap off, bent down, and dunked it in the stream. Then he put the wet cap back on his head, and let water trickle down his face and shoulders. "Ah! Ice-cold mountain water," he said.

Kaitlyn knelt down beside him. She cupped her hands in the water and splashed her face. Then she opened her eyes. "Dad, look!" she exclaimed.

Dad looked down. "Whoa!" His eyes lit up. Next to the water were the paw prints of a large animal.

"They look like dog prints," said Kaitlyn.

"There are no dogs up here, Kaitlyn. They aren't allowed on the trails." Dad crouched down to study the print. "These are too big for a coyote. I think they belong to …"

"A wolf?" Kaitlyn interrupted.

"It sure looks like it." Dad stood up. "I don't know how it could be, though. For years, biologists have been talking about bringing wolves back to the park. But they haven't. It's too controversial."

"Why?" Kaitlyn asked.

"People think that wolves are bad. They believe that wolves kill cattle and hurt people. Really – wolves aren't like that. They don't usually come near people. And if they *did* come back to the park, they'd find plenty of wildlife to eat, so they wouldn't need to attack farmers' cattle."

"Let's take a picture of the prints," Kaitlyn suggested.

"Good idea," Dad agreed. "I'll take the picture. Put your foot next to one of the prints so we'll remember how big they are."

Kaitlyn took the camera from around her neck and gave it to Dad. He stood up on a large rock and focused the camera on Kaitlyn's foot and the animal print. He adjusted the zoom lens, then took a step back. He adjusted the lens further. He leaned back and put his finger on the button.

The rock suddenly tipped. *"Ahhhh!"* Dad shouted as he fell backward.

"Dad!" Kaitlyn screamed as she watched him roll downhill. He tumbled through some bushes, and into a tree. *Blam!*

Dad lay still for a few seconds, then slowly stood up. He still had his pack, but he had dropped the camera in the bushes. He walked over to retrieve it.

As he bent over to pick it up, he gasped. "I don't believe it!" he whispered to himself.

"Dad! Are you okay?" Kaitlyn shouted down to him.

Dad looked up. "I'm fine. But can you get down here? I want you to see this!"

: ## CHAPTER 6

Return of the Wolf?

Kaitlyn scrambled down the hill and joined her father.

"Look at this." Dad pointed out several bones on the ground. "These look like deer bones. And they've been chewed on."

Kaitlyn looked at the bones, then glanced at the whole area. The grass was matted down, and dirt was flung out in a pile. "It looks as if someone has been here before."

"Absolutely!" Dad said. "But not some*one* – some*thing*."

"Wolves?" Kaitlyn asked.

"Yes. I'm positive now." Dad put all the pieces together. "You said you heard howling last night – howling, right? Not yipping?"

Kaitlyn nodded.

"We saw fresh droppings on top of the mountain," Dad continued. "And it did seem awfully large for a coyote. Then we saw a wolf print along the trail. And now these deer bones. I'll bet it was a wolf that ate this deer. Coyotes sometimes hunt deer, but they're less likely to go after the big animals."

Dad pointed toward the base of a nearby tree. "Now look at this!"

Kaitlyn saw a number of large holes under the tree's roots. "What are those?" she asked.

"I think it's a wolf den."

Kaitlyn gulped. "A wolf den? Do you think there are wolves in there?"

"I think we'd hear them if they were there," Dad answered. "It's July. The pups should be old enough to head out with their parents to hunt. Who knows? Maybe they're on their way back. Or maybe they're watching us – waiting for us to leave."

Kaitlyn stood up and looked all around. She moved closer to Dad, and whispered, "Maybe we should get out of here."

"Don't worry," said Dad. "They won't hurt us. But you're right, we should leave. This is their home, not ours."

Dad snapped a photo of the den and the deer bones. Then he and Kaitlyn scrambled up the hill and back onto the trail. Once there, Dad and Kaitlyn stood still for a moment to listen. There was not a sound. They headed down the trail and back to their camp, hoping to arrive before dark.

CHAPTER 7

Stargazing

That night, after dinner, Dad gazed in awe at the twinkling sky. "Just look at all those stars," he said.

"We don't get to see this where we live, huh, Dad?" Kaitlyn responded. "Can we come back here next summer?"

"You bet!" Dad answered. "Who knows? When I show our photographs to some of the biologists at the park, they might ask us to come back and help the rangers to track and observe the wolves."

"That would be neat!" Kaitlyn exclaimed.

Dad and Kaitlyn fell silent. They walked back and forth from the campfire to their backpacks, putting food away. As soon as the backpacks were zipped up, Dad looped a rope through them. He tossed the other end of the rope over a tree branch. Dad tugged on the rope and hoisted the packs high off the ground – and away from the tree's trunk. Then he tied the excess rope around a rock.

"That'll keep the bears out," Dad said. He walked over to the tent. Kaitlyn was already inside. "Are you asleep?"

"Not yet," Kaitlyn answered.

Dad crawled inside the tent and zipped it up. He wriggled into his sleeping bag.

"I'm glad I came here," Kaitlyn said.

"I knew you'd like it," Dad answered.

"I do," Kaitlyn went on. "I'm glad the wolves came back."

"Me too," answered Dad. "It's the best thing that's happened to the park in ages."

"I hope they stay here and have lots of pups," said Kaitlyn.

"That would be great," Dad replied. He yawned. "It's a shame we can't stay longer. But we still have all day tomorrow to see the rest of the park, so we'd better get some sleep. Good night, Kaitlyn."

"Good night, Dad."

CHAPTER 8

Once in a Lifetime

*A*h *ooooo ... oooo... Ah oooooooooo ...*

Kaitlyn woke up.

Ah ooooo ... A wolf howled from across the valley.

"Is that what you heard last night?" Dad whispered.

"Yep. That's it," Kaitlyn answered, glad that Dad was awake this time.

Ah ooooo ... Another wolf howled.

Dad sat up. "Those are definitely wolves." He turned over and grabbed two flashlights from the side of the tent. "Come on, get your shoes on."

"You mean we're going out *there*?" Kaitlyn asked.

"We won't go far," said Dad, as he handed Kaitlyn a flashlight.

Dad and Kaitlyn turned on their flashlights, unzipped the tent, and climbed out. Kaitlyn shivered. "It's cold out here!"

Dad reached back into the tent and grabbed their jackets. They put them on as they walked over to the campfire. Dad stirred the coals until they glowed. He tossed some wood in the ring. The coals ignited, and there was a small fire again. Dad and Kaitlyn sat and waited.

Ah ooooo … Ah ooooo … The wolves howled to each other. The sound seemed to be getting closer.

Dad and Kaitlyn shone their flashlights into the forest around them. It was silent for a moment.

Kaitlyn moved closer to her father. "Look!" she whispered.

At the edge of the forest, a pair of eyes shone in the firelight. A lone gray wolf strutted toward the campfire. It stood a short distance from Dad and Kaitlyn.

"Dad!" Kaitlyn whispered. "What should we do?"

"Nothing," Dad answered. "We'll be okay. Just stay still."

29

Two smaller wolves trotted out of the forest, and nuzzled up to the adult.

Kaitlyn held on to Dad's arm, and whispered, "Wolf pups!" Kaitlyn's heart was pounding.

"We're glad you're back," Dad said softly. "The park has missed you."

The adult wolf looked at Dad and tilted its head. The pups hid behind the adult.

Ah ooooo ... A wolf howled deep in the forest.

The adult wolf stretched its neck upward and lifted its head toward the moon. *Ah ooooooooo* ... *Ah ooooooooo* ...

Dad and Kaitlyn stared in awe.

Ah ooooo ... The other wolf howled again in the forest.

The pups chimed in. *Ow! Ow! Ow!* They barked and yelped. *Ow! Ow! Ow! Ow!*

The adult wolf perked up its ears. It looked into the woods, then back at Dad and Kaitlyn. Then it turned and trotted back into the darkness of the forest. The two pups followed close behind.

"Wow!" Dad gasped. "We are *very* lucky to see wolves that close. That's a once-in-a-lifetime experience."

"That was so cool!" Kaitlyn agreed.

Dad and Kaitlyn sat next to the fire for a few minutes, hoping that the wolves would come back. As the fire slowly died, the air felt chillier.

Dad stood up. "Come on, Kaitlyn. It's time to get some sleep."

"Okay." Kaitlyn stood up and followed her father. As they walked back to the tent, she turned to look back into the dark forest once more. She saw thousands of stars in the sky, and the silhouettes of the trees lit by moonlight. But no wolves.

As she turned again to head back to the tent, Kaitlyn heard a familiar sound echoing through the forest.

Ah ooooo ... ooo ... Ah ooooo ... ooo ...